SOLAR SYSTEM

by Gregory Vogt

SCHOLASTIC INC.

New York   Toronto   London   Sydney
Auckland   Mexico City   New Delhi   Hong Kong

ISBN 978-0-545-38267-0

10 9   13 14 15 16/0
Printed in the U.S.A.   40
This edition first printing, January 2012

We live on a **planet** called Earth.
Earth belongs to a very large family of
eight planets and more than 150 **moons**.
The entire family is known as the
solar system.

THE SUN

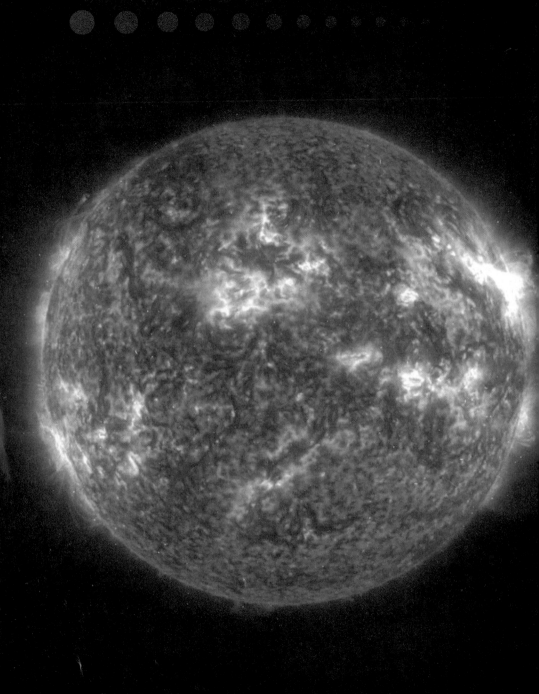

At night, we see many **stars**. During the day, we see only one—the Sun. The Sun looks much larger because it is millions of times closer to us. In fact, the Sun is the center of the solar system.

The Sun has **gravity** (grav-i-tee). Gravity is a force that attracts objects to one another. The Sun's gravity pulls on the planets and forces them to travel around it. They follow paths called **orbits**. The Sun's gravity keeps the solar system together.

SUN ● ● ● ● ● ● ● ● ●

Size Across:	864,970 miles (1,392,000 kilometers)
Rotation: (one complete spin)	24 to 34 days (The Sun's middle spins faster than its north and south poles.)
Composition:	Hydrogen, Helium
Temperature:	Surface: 6,400° F (3,571° C) Center: 15,000,000° F (8,333,316° C)

MERCURY

Mercury is the closest planet to the Sun. The side of Mercury facing the Sun gets twice as hot as a kitchen oven—800º F (427º C).

Mercury is a rocky planet. There are thousands of bowl-shaped holes called craters on its surface. These craters were made when **meteors** (mee-tee-urs) smashed into Mercury.

MERCURY

Size Across:	3,031 miles (4,880 kilometers)
Distance from the Sun:	35,340,000 miles (56,872,662 kilometers)
Orbit Length: (once around the Sun)	87.97 days
Rotation:	58.64 days
Number of Moons:	None
Number of Rings:	None

VENUS

The second planet from the Sun is Venus. It is nearly as large as Earth. Venus is covered with thick clouds. The Sun's heat passes through these clouds and gets trapped at the surface. The trapped heat makes Venus the hottest planet.

Venus is made of rock from volcanoes. Its surface is covered with lava. How do we know about Venus when we can't see its surface? **Astronomers** (uh-strah-nuh-mers), scientists who study space, use spacecrafts to learn about Venus.

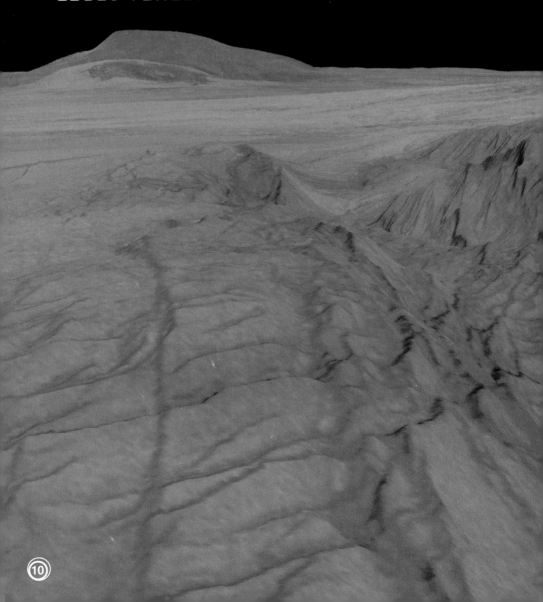

VENUS

Size Across:	7,520 miles (12,102 kilometers)
Distance from the Sun:	67,239,000 miles (108,207,000 kilometers)
Orbit Length: (once around the Sun)	224.7 days
Rotation:	243 days
Number of Moons:	None
Number of Rings:	None

EARTH

● ● ● ● ● ● ● ● ● ● ● ● ● ●

Earth is the third planet from
the Sun. It is mostly covered with
water. Earth is home to billions of
plants and animals. There is life
nearly everywhere you look.

Earth is constantly changing. Winds blow across the surface. Water runs across the land and wears it away. Volcanoes spew lava and make new land.

EARTH

Size Across:	7,916 miles (12,742 kilometers)
Distance from the Sun:	93,000,000 miles (149,000,000 kilometers)
Orbit Length: (once around the Sun)	1 year
Rotation:	24 hours
Number of Moons:	1
Number of Rings:	None

EARTH'S MOON

The Moon is made of rocks from volcanoes. Sunlight bouncing off its surface makes it look white.

In 1969, the first humans landed on the Moon. These **astronauts** (as-truh-nawts) returned with moon rocks. Then astronomers studied the rocks to learn about the Moon.

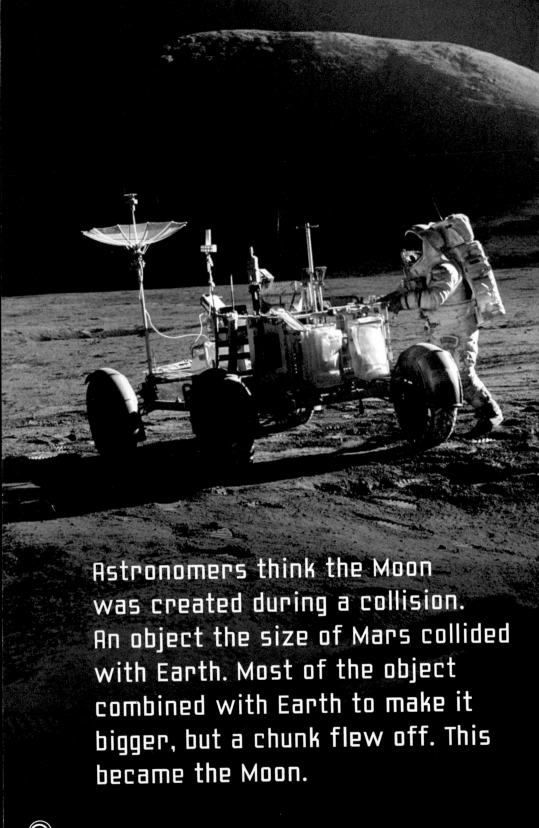

Astronomers think the Moon
was created during a collision.
An object the size of Mars collided
with Earth. Most of the object
combined with Earth to make it
bigger, but a chunk flew off. This
became the Moon.

MARS

● ● ● ● ● ● ● ● ● · ·

Mars, the fourth planet from the Sun, is reddish. Its surface is covered with rust-colored rocks and dust.

Olympus Mons

Mars also has very large volcanoes. The volcano Olympus Mons is three times taller than Mount Everest on Earth.

Mars has a thin **atmosphere** (at-muhs-feer) surrounding it, but there is not enough air for humans to breathe. If you went there, you would have to wear a space suit.

MARS

Size Across:	4,212 miles (6,794 kilometers)
Distance from the Sun:	141,637,725 miles (228,089,300 kilometers)
Orbit Length: (once around the Sun)	1.88 years
Rotation:	24.62 hours
Number of Moons:	Two
Number of Rings:	None

JUPITER

Jupiter is the fifth planet from the Sun. It is the largest planet and is nearly eleven times wider than Earth. It is made of gas.

Great Red Spot

Jupiter has a huge storm that swirls like a hurricane. The storm itself is twice the size of Earth. Astronomers have named it the Great Red Spot.

JUPITER ● ● ● ● ● ● ●

Size Across:	86,880 miles (139,822 kilometers)
Distance from the Sun:	483,638,564 miles (778,340,821 kilometers)
Orbit Length: (once around the Sun)	11.86 years
Rotation:	9.92 hours
Number of Moons:	50
Number of Rings:	3

SATURN

Saturn is the sixth planet from the Sun. It has thousands of narrow rings circling it. The rings are made of rocks, ice, and dust.

More than fifty moons orbit Saturn. Astronomers keep discovering more. One moon, Titan, is wider than Mercury.

SATURN

Size Across:	72,366 miles (116,464 kilometers)
Distance from the Sun:	886,489, 415 miles (1,426,666,422 kilometers)
Orbit Length: (once around the Sun)	29.44 years
Rotation:	10.66 hours
Number of Moons:	53
Number of Rings:	Thousands

URANUS

Uranus is the seventh planet from the Sun. Uranus is four times larger than Earth. Chemicals in the air make the planet look blue.

Uranus is a sideways planet. It spins like all planets but it is tilted on its side. For half of its orbit, Uranus's north pole points toward the Sun. For the other half, the south pole points toward the Sun.

URANUS

Size Across:	31,518 miles (50, 724 kilometers)
Distance from the Sun:	1,868,039,489 miles (3,006,318,143 kilometers)
Orbit Length: (once around the Sun)	84.01 years
Rotation:	17.24 hours
Number of Moons:	27
Number of Rings:	13

NEPTUNE

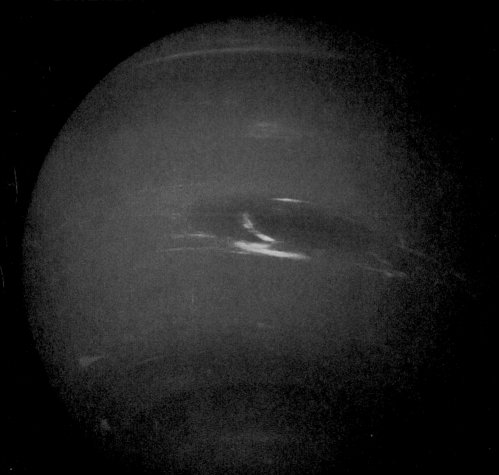

Neptune is the eighth planet from the Sun. It is blue in color and about as large as Uranus. Neptune has storms like Jupiter's, but they are smaller.

Neptune has several moons. The biggest is Triton. Astronomers have noticed that Triton is getting closer to Neptune. Millions of years from now, Triton could crash into Neptune.

NEPTUNE

Size Across:	30,598 miles (49,244 kilometers)
Distance from the Sun:	2,819,185,846 miles (4,537,039,826 kilometers)
Orbit Length: (once around the Sun)	164.8 years
Rotation:	16.11 hours
Number of Moons:	13
Number of Rings:	9

ASTEROIDS

Thousands of **asteroids** (as-tuh-roids) orbit the Sun. These rocks can be hundreds of miles across or the size of a house. Many asteroids orbit the Sun between Mars and Jupiter.

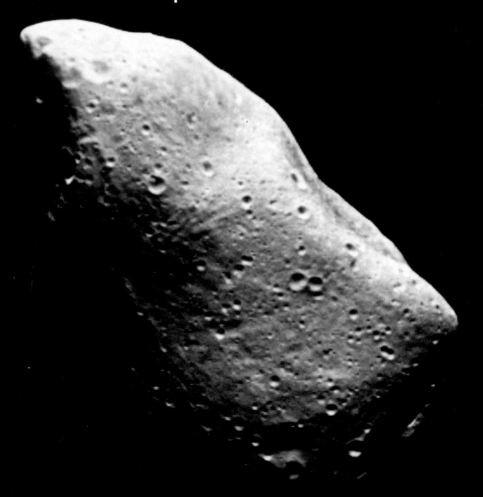

COMETS

● ● ● ● ● ● ● ● ● ● ● ●

Far beyond Neptune are billions of chunks of ice called **comets** (kah-mits). Comets are usually a few miles wide. Sometimes, a comet is bumped toward the Sun. The Sun's heat starts melting the ice. A long white tail of gas streaks out for millions of miles.

GLOSSARY

Asteroids . . . . large pieces of space rock

Astronomer . . . a scientist who studies objects in outer space

Astronaut . . . . someone who travels into outer space

Atmosphere . . the mixture of gases that surrounds a planet

Comets . . . . . . large balls of ice that form long tails when they near the Sun

Gravity . . . . . . the force that attracts all objects to one another

Meteors . . . . . pieces of rock or metal from space that fall to a planet

Moons . . . . balls of rock or ice that orbit planets

Orbits . . . . the paths planets travel around the Sun

Planet . . . . a large ball of rock or gas that orbits the Sun

Solar system . . the family of the Sun, planets, moons, asteroids, and comets

Stars . . . . huge balls of very hot gas